Fiscally and Physically Fit for Life

Fiscally and Physically Fit for Life

Geoff Fellows and Vince Levigne

Columbus, Ohio

The views and opinions expressed in this book are solely those of the author and do not reflect the views or opinions of Gatekeeper Press. Gatekeeper Press is not to be held responsible for and expressly disclaims responsibility of the content herein.

Fiscally and Physically Fit for Life

Published by Gatekeeper Press
2167 Stringtown Rd, Suite 109
Columbus, OH 43123-2989
www.GatekeeperPress.com

Copyright © 2020 by Geoff Fellows and Vince Levigne, and contributor, Jennifer Yeh
All rights reserved. Neither this book, nor any parts within it may be sold or reproduced in any form or by any electronic or mechanical means, including information storage and retrieval systems without permission in writing from the author. The only exception is by a reviewer, who may quote short excerpts in a review.

ISBN (paperback): 9781662902000
eISBN: 9781662902017

Library of Congress Control Number: 2020940170

Contents

Foreword vii

Chapter 1	It's All Really Easy	1
Chapter 2	The Benefits of Working With a Professional	7
Chapter 3	Picking the Right Professional	17
Chapter 4	Starting Early: Pay It Now or Pay It Later	23
Chapter 5	Getting Started	29
Chapter 6	Beginner Level	35
Chapter 7	Intermediate Level	41
Chapter 8	Advanced Level	47
Chapter 9	Expert Level	59
Chapter 10	Other Investments: Real Estate and Annuities	67

Chapter 11	Beware the Get-Rich-Quick Schemes	75
Chapter 12	Pulling it All Together	83
The Boldface Summary		87
Citations		89
About the Authors		95

Foreword

A quick note about how to read this book right from the beginning. "Fiscally and Physically Fit For Life" is not intended to be a college-level finance (or fitness) book, in that you won't need to know how to create Excel spreadsheets, be expected to calculate Black-Scholes Options Pricing equations in your head, or for that matter have a working knowledge of the skeletal muscular structure of the human body. In many regards, we have simplified most concepts down to straight-forward explanations and demonstrated those explanations through stories and examples. Some chapters are short, others are longer. That being said, this book is intended to give you a working knowledge of investing and investments (and fitness) just powerful enough to make you dangerous. Remember, there are always deeper nuances to almost every concept that we discuss and you should be aware those nuances do exist.

This book is intended to be read in the order that the chapters appear. Sure, we can't stop you from flipping ahead to the chapters that seem interesting, however, each chapter builds off the ones before it, and diving into the middle of the book is like diving into the middle of a recipe, what you get out of it may not be what you intended. However, once you have read the entire book, if at some point you want to go back and refresh yourself on a concept, you will at least understand how that concept fits into the greater scheme of investing or fitness and be able to get what you need. Each chapter ends with an 'Easy Learning' summary. At the end of the book, we have included a collection of all the Chapter Summaries for quick reference.

Throughout this book, you may find words in **BOLD** the first time they appear. While most of these words are known to you, if we have used those words in a specific way (or think they are worth remembering), we have called them out – and provided a quick definition as we use the word so we can build on them later. The definitions are simplified for ease of understanding, and we recognize that experts in the field may critique that we have been overly simplistic. The fact is, if we wrote a book to satisfy those experts' curiosity, it would be a totally different book and we knowingly accept that responsibility.

Finally, the lawyers have told us that we need to remind you that these pages represent our own beliefs

Foreword

and assertions and do not represent the opinions, guidance, or positions (legal or otherwise) of any of our associates, the people or organizations that we work for, with, or represent. Any fault you find with these pages is our own.

Geoff and Vince

Chapter 1

It's All Really Easy

Have you ever opened a box from a Swedish furniture store, read the instructions, and then packed everything back up and taken the box back to the store? Maybe you have looked at the back of your television set with wires for the cable service, the DVR, and the gaming console; then shook your head in disbelief and closed your eyes. How many of you once owned VCRs whose clock flashed "00:00" for the life of the machine? Most people have, and if you did, Vince and I are here to tell you that you are not alone in your reactions. Life is full of things that are supposed to be easy, but when we dive into them (heck, when we just lightly scratch the surface), they get complicated very fast.

When it comes to saving and investing (or physical fitness), most people experience exactly the same spectrum of feelings. One day some random event fires us up, we quickly get great intentions and open the 'furniture box' to find that there are no instructions. At this point, most smart people pack everything back up in the box and set it on the 'mental' shelf to be dealt with in the future. Unfortunately, that box often sits on the shelf until many years later when we want to either buy a house, send our kids to college, retire, or what began as a nagging pain has become a chronic medical issue... but by then, it's often too late to do anything about it.

Don't believe it? Let's look at some statistics:

- In the 1960s, Americans saved on average over 11.0% of their salaries. In the last decade, that number fell to less than 7.6% – at the same time, the inflation rate averaged 3.94%.[1]
- In the late 1990s, more than 60% of Americans reported that they owned **STOCK** (a representation of corporate ownership – historically in paper certificate form but now held electronically. If a company issues 100 shares of stock then 1 share would equal 1.0% ownership), but even with the rampant proliferation of 401(k)s, by 2019 that number had fallen into the low 50% range.[2]
- Homeownership (most Americans' single largest investment) fell from a peak of nearly 70% at the beginning of the millennium to almost 65% by last year and the trends indicate it will go lower with many feeling they are being priced out of the market.[3]

- A CNBC poll conducted at the end of 2019 shows that 7 out of 10 Americans wished they had handled their money differently.[4]

There are many reasons for these numbers. For example, many millennials value the freedom that renting affords. The ability to pick up and move at the end of the lease, either for their job or just for a change of scenery, makes the anchor of homeownership less appealing. For our parents and grandparents, owning their own home was the ultimate American dream.

While recent average merit increases have hovered around 3.5%[5], inflation (mentioned above) eats into this growth, making many of us feel like we just aren't getting ahead fast enough. At the same time, the growth in the number of ways to save or invest has exploded. Online accounts, credit cards that round up purchases to place the excess in savings, cell phone applications that allow us to buy pieces of fractions of shares instantly, and complex **DERIVATIVES** (an investment class that creates value from a number of often unrelated alternative investments) that promise high returns and quick gains are all set against stories of unscrupulous 'billionaire' scam artists and applications that disappear from our cell phones overnight. When our parents, educators, or society haven't effectively taught us how to save, it's easy to get overwhelmed quickly, pack everything back up in that mental box, and put it on the shelf until later.

Changing gears for a moment, how many of us have picked up a couple extra pounds as we've gotten older? Maybe our knees are starting to ache when it rains, our backs are beginning to get sore when we play with the kids, and our layups on the basketball court seem to have lost a step. Great intentions lead us to the door of the local gym, where we stand staring at rows of machines straight out of a medieval horror story, and muscle-bound gym regulars are throwing around what seems to be enough weight to rival a herd of small elephants. The smell is overwhelming, and the cherry Danish pastry and caramel macchiato latte at the coffee shop across the street quickly looks like a much wiser investment of our time.

We laughed, but the numbers bear it out. **OBESITY** (having a body mass index of greater than 28) in men and women has gone from approximately 11% and 15% respectively in 1960 to 35% and 40% respectively in 2015. Cardiovascular-related diseases are responsible for nearly 31% of annual deaths in the United States. Add in cancers and the combined totals approach 60%.[6]

With fitness, we generally don't pack up our mental box quite as easily. Many Americans shift to Plan B and go shopping on the internet for alternatives. Thus, we have a stunning range of products from electrodes that will electrocute our abdominal muscles, to dumbbells that will vibrate on their own, to stationary bicycles costing as much as our first car – all promising to make us look lean and hot in our summer outfits.

The underlying problems between understanding fiscal and physical fitness are very much the same. Too much information, too many seemingly complicated choices, and too many products that can hurt us if we don't know how to use them properly. All of these coupled with the fact that no one has really taught us how to be either fiscally or physically fit leads most of us to set the issue aside – to pack up that mental box – and deal with it later... often when it's too late.

Let's go back to our Swedish furniture example for a moment. Have you ever watched in awe as a friend rips open the box, throws away the instructions, and assembles the piece in minutes? Maybe you watched a YouTube video and 5 minutes later... bam! ... the scantily clad, attractive star had it all put together without all the extra screws, nuts, and unidentifiable pieces left over.

What if someone told you that both fiscal and physical fitness were actually pretty simple? First, you'd probably scoff. Then, you would probably throw this book out. We aren't going to do that. But we are going to share some simple, easy-to-understand guidance – like the YouTube furniture assembly video – that will put all of us on the path to a good, solid fiscal and physical fitness regimen. We won't be trading copper **FUTURES** (a type of investment) hedged with **FOREIGN EXCHANGE ARBITRAGE** (another type of investment) or competing in Olympic events after reading it, but it will give us the fundamentals that we need to set ourselves up to develop healthy habits on our own.

So here is the first Easy Learning (1 for our fiscal fitness and 1 for our physical fitness):

1. *Fiscal – To save money, we MUST spend less than we make.*
1. *Physical – To lose weight, we MUST burn more calories than we consume.*

CHAPTER 2

The Benefits of Working With a Professional

If we went to a world-renowned doctor with a sore elbow, we would expect the doctor to fix the elbow pain. We would probably be expecting an x-ray, possibly a sling, and definitely some medication. None of us goes to the doctor for a sore elbow and expects to be cured of every single ache and pain, allowing us to live forever.

If we went to a highly-priced attorney for a speeding ticket, we would likely expect to go to court. Realistically, we would hope to get off with a reduced fine, potentially some traffic school, and, with luck, no points on our driving record. Not one of us expects to go to an attorney for a speeding ticket and to have our will or trust drafted, our neighbor's dog enjoined from barking before 8:00 am on Sundays, and the ticket resolved in one session.

In fact, none of us expect our semi-skilled gardener to plant the flower beds and mow the lawn so that the blooms will never die and the lawn will never go brown. Yet when many people walk into a **FINANCIAL ADVISOR**'s *[we are speaking of a licensed, regulated, and competent professional that will help you make investment decisions to accomplish future goals]* office (or the gym for that matter), all reason seems to get left in the car.

When clients come into our offices, one of the first questions both Vince and I always ask is: What are your expectations? Too often the response is one that would make a less professional person laugh. One prospective client wanted to double their money by the week's end. Another felt that their $5,000 investment should be worth close to $1 million by the year's end. In the fitness world, a third client came into the gym looking for ways to shed 100 lbs in a month, while yet another wanted to add 50 lbs to his bench press in 2 weeks. You think we jest. Sadly, we don't.

Realistic savings and investing (and physical fitness) expectations are about having a documented, diversified, and disciplined action plan, the "3 D's." Let's look at each of those concepts a little deeper.

DOCUMENTATION

Let's face it, none of us is as young as we once were, and as we age the mental cobwebs get a little thicker. When I asked my co-author what he had for breakfast this morning – he couldn't remember. Not that **NUTRITION** (Nutrition is more than just the foods we eat or the number of calories we consume – it encompasses a calorie and substance plan applicable to the fitness goals we are trying to accomplish) isn't extremely important to him, but it is one of the million new facts that we encounter in a day that gets stored in our brains and ranks pretty low on the scale of things we NEED to remember. Savings and investing (and fitness) on the other hand rank way up at the top of that scale...pretty darned important.

Documentation works to assist the memory in two very important ways: A) At some point during the journey, we are going to want to recall what decision was made and/or why that decision was made and B) We'll undoubtedly want to know what to do when the professional isn't around to coach us.

Why we are investing is important to keep at the top of our minds. Is this investment to fund retirement 30 years from now? That's a long time to keep focused. Is it to buy a house in 5 years? When our friends want to go to Las Vegas for the weekend, that down payment for a house can be the furthest thing from our mind. Having that "Why" goal front and center every time we look at our investments helps keep us laser-focused on the game plan.

We also want to document the WHAT we are investing in. Have you ever opened your closet and found a shirt that is as ugly as a crime? You might have wondered to yourself "what was I thinking when I bought this?" More than one investor has looked into their portfolio and asked the same question: What was I thinking when I bought that? Having a cheat sheet to remind us that we needed a position in the health care **SECTOR,** or we needed a **DIVIDEND** payer to create some income, or we took a flyer on an educated guess quickly jogs the memory.

Documentation also helps us remember what to do when the professional isn't at our elbow coaching our every move. Great investors religiously contribute a portion of their weekly salaries, annual bonuses, or merit increases into their portfolio. Remembering how much to put into an **INDIVIDUAL RETIREMENT ACCOUNT (IRA)** (an investment account that affords special tax treatment like a personal 401(k)) or how to fill in the tax paperwork on the lottery windfall can allow us to operate as knowledgeable investors without having to be babysat through the process. Let's face it, investing is about gaining control over our future financial choices, no one likes to have a babysitter.

I tell my clients that they should A) have a **FINANCIAL PLAN** (a documented plan outlining our goals, the expected time horizons, required returns, tax strategies, and risk profile with an indicator of how well our actual performance is tracking against those objectives) and B) put a copy of that plan under their bed AND a copy in their golf bag. It's not something we need to re-read every day. It's usually at night before sleep that doubt overtakes us, or on the golf course when a buddy starts talking about a friend of a friend who invested in this or that get-rich-quick scheme, that having our plan right there in front of us can keep us from making an emotional decision and keep us focused on the educated decisions.

In the gym, the most serious of athletes always have a game plan. We bet you've never seen a professional athlete walk into a gym and stare in confusion over what workout they want to do. We will likely see them put in their earphones and 'zone out', focused on accomplishing their objectives. These athletes know the day's workout is going to focus on **STRENGTH, ENDURANCE,** or **FLEXIBILITY** to improve their total performance. Most likely that plan was written out well in advance of the morning's visit. The same athletes also regularly document their workouts, so they can measure their improvement over time. By learning and using the tools in this book, we as investors are becoming pro-athletes in the marathon of our financial lives.

DIVERSIFICATION

The old adage 'don't keep all your eggs in one basket' literally is THE watchword of any good investment portfolio. We once had a client tell us that he owned shares of Apple stock in his 401(k) at his company, his investment account, and his IRA that he held with me, and another IRA that he held at another firm.

He felt strongly that he had spread his eggs over many baskets and wasn't in danger of losing anything if any one of us went out of business. After a deep and very disapproving sigh, we explained to the client that he had diversified against his advisors going out of business, but what if Apple went out of business?

Another client whose paycheck came from a very large company with local offices here in Southern California explained to me that he was making great retirement investment decisions because every time his company offered its employees the option to buy company stock at a discount, he jumped on it and sank every free penny he had into the purchase. As you can imagine, another deep and disapproving sigh emanated, followed by the explanation that the client had tied not only his current income to the success of the company, but he had also tied his entire retirement plan to the company's continued success.

Diversification means spreading risk so when some things go down, hopefully others are going up. Spreading our portfolio risk over different sectors of the economy, different types of investments, and with different investing objectives is the surest way to avoid a single unexpected event destroying all the value in our portfolio. That doesn't mean we need to own everything, which is what many first-time investors who have heard of diversification want to do. A smaller portfolio over three different investments may be as appropriate as a larger portfolio over twenty investments.

The Benefits of Working With a Professional

I met my co-author when I was re-habilitating my blown-out knee. That is a long story for another book, but let us just say a freak golf swing took me down. I wanted the best specialist money could buy and I found Vince relatively close to my home base. In the 6 years since he worked my knee back into shape, we have become great friends and regularly work out together in the mornings before my market opens and his clients have even dreamed of their first cup of coffee.

That opportunity has afforded us the chance to see many people come and go through the gym and I am reminded of one guy who came to the gym as regularly as we did. Every day he did the same **UPPER BODY** and arm exercises. Over time, the amount of weight he could lift grew impressively heavier. His size increased as well until his arms were as big around as my thighs. Unfortunately, because he only worked his chest and arms, this individual's thighs stayed the same puny size as when he started, and now whenever Vince or I want to skip leg day... we remind each other of the "bulging biceps with a side order of chicken legs." The moral being, you have to vary your workout or you may end up funny looking.

DISCIPLINE

If in real estate it's "Location! Location! Location!," then in both investing and the gym its "Discipline! Discipline! Discipline!" It is about having the discipline to start early, the discipline to stay investing through the tough times, and the discipline to stick to the game plan.

Starting early can mean getting an early start to the day, but here we specifically mean starting earlier in life. You have to admit the day before you retire is not the time to try and build an investment portfolio, nor is the day before our first heart attack the day to start exercising.

By way of demonstration, let us share with you the story of two friends who we will call Fred and Barney. Both are 22 years old and freshly graduated from university.

Fred starts early, putting $500 into his IRA every month, starting from the first day of his new job. $500 a month over 12 months is $6,000 (the current legal contribution limit to an IRA for a 22-year-old). He does this for 10 years for a total of $60,000 of his own money and then NEVER invests another penny. Now, Fred has to make sacrifices to put away this money at an entry-level salary, but he foregoes the new car and the exotic vacations and stays disciplined.

Barney on the other hand takes 10 years to play. Spending every last dime (never going into debt mind you) but not denying himself anything he wants. When Barney turns 32, he starts the same $500 a month, $6,000 a year. But he saves for 33 years until he turns 65, saving $198,000 of his salary over that time.

If both Fred and Barney achieve the exact same performance (say an average 7% return), Barney will have an impressive $823,000 saved in his IRA. But Fred, who started early, stayed at it when it was hard, and stuck to the game plan, will have an amazing $945,000. Who would you rather be?[1]

When it comes to your physical fitness, the same story applies. Good health habits established early will reap benefits for years to come and may forestall the effects of aging.[2]

Of course, going to the gym with a buddy is a lot more fun than dragging ourselves on our own. But, many people working out in the gym have established and repeated their exercise routines from something their high school coach taught them, something they saw online, or from watching someone else in the gym. There are many possible things that can go wrong in all of those scenarios. Are we working the right joints and muscles for our age or physical ability? What we *could* do in high school is often well beyond what we *should* be doing in middle age.

Does our gym partner prepare our body for exercise with stretching and warm-up light-weight or body-weight exercises? An industry study suggests that over 75% of injuries (major and minor) come from an improper warm-up.[3] Muscles get torn, joints get damaged, and egos get bruised. Does our gym buddy apply safe **Frequency Intensity Time under tension and Type training (FITT)** principles to the routine? Alternate exercise to different regions of the body to prevent fatigue or injury? Teach us how to utilize equipment for maximum efficiency? A personal trainer can customize a workout plan for our specific needs, monitor our progress through that routine, and adjust the plan as necessary to accomplish the goals we have established for ourselves.

More than one legitimate university study shows that working with a financial advisor helps the average investor achieve 3.0% better return than investing on your own – because that advisor A) helps us establish and document a plan that keeps us on track, B) brings access to information and knowledge ahead of the general public, allowing us to diversify and position ourselves better than the average person watching the evening news, and C) takes the emotion out of the investment decisions; keeping us in when the market dips and getting us out when the market crests.[4]

Chapter 2 Easy Learning concepts:

2. *Fiscal – The 3 D's and a professional financial advisor can help us reach our investing goals.*
2. *Physical – The 3 D's and a professional certified trainer can help us achieve our health goals.*

CHAPTER 3

Picking the Right Professional

Have you ever seen the commercial from Holiday Inn, where the actor looks into the camera and says, "I'm not a doctor, but I stayed at a Holiday Inn last night."[1] The implication is that while the actor may not be medically qualified to cure our ills, we can at least rest assured that he makes good decisions when it comes to staying at hotels. When it comes to picking the right professional to work with, that commercial should be playing in the back of our minds. There are professionals and then there are Professionals.

There is a dirty little secret in the Financial Advisor space, and that is: almost anyone can call themselves a Financial Advisor or Financial Planner. Anyone who has sat through a 60-hour course on Life and Health Insurance (52 hours in California with Ethics) with the variable annuity add-on (8 hours in California) is legally qualified to call themselves a Financial Advisor, because they are legally allowed to sell us products that in many ways resemble investments.[2] There are many accountants, lawyers, and even teachers on summer break who are willing to sit through the class and will tell us that all our financial needs can be addressed with a single insurance product (see annuities discussed in Chapter 10). Without exception, those products pay the seller very handsomely.

On the other end of the spectrum, the Certified Financial Planner (CFP) organization has a multi-million dollar a year marketing campaign in print, on TV, and on the radio to convince you that the *only* qualified Financial Advisor must have the CFP stamp of approval.[3] While requiring additional training, a minimum of 3 years of industry experience, and passing a test, that designation proves little more than that the Advisor is willing to pay the annual dues. We personally know many CFPs who promptly forgot everything they learned immediately after they passed the CFP qualification exam. There are many Advisors between these two ends of the spectrum who are qualified, knowledgeable, and good at what they do. Brokers, Registered Investment Representatives, Registered Investment Advisors, and Wealth Managers all maintain some of the highest levels of qualifications and licensing. Don't let titles or exotic-sounding designations fool you.

When selecting the financial advisor we want to work with, there are only two critical pieces of information that we should consider: what is that advisor's investment philosophy? And are they a **FIDUCIARY**? If we are conservative by nature, an aggressively investing advisor will be unlikely to fit our personality. Conversely, if we are looking to be aggressive, a conservative advisor most likely won't meet our needs either. Lastly, some advisors don't really make any of the investment decisions themselves. They allow someone at headquarters or a third-party investment manager to take the responsibility for choosing the investments and really only serve as a sales funnel to those investment managers. We should select an advisor that matches our own philosophy on investing and will be able to answer our questions as to why they are recommending this investment over that one.

A Fiduciary is a relatively new term in the financial advice space, so much so that the exact definition hasn't even been hammered out in the regulations yet.[4] However, the concept has been around for a long time, and it means that the person we pay for advice will not only morally, but legally put our interests before their own. Do we want to be wondering every day whether the person managing our investments is making more money than we are? Would that color how we view their advice? Likely, the answer is yes. Thus, selecting an advisor that is willing to enter a Fiduciary relationship with us is important to assure that the person we pay is working for us.

In the fitness field, the problem is the same. Some people who know how to spell the word "gym" call themselves Trainers. Just because they know how to work a particular piece of gym equipment doesn't mean that they can help us achieve our fitness goals. More importantly, they do not necessarily know how to develop a fitness routine that won't hurt us.

The internet is full of self-proclaimed fitness experts, sports trainers, and healthy-living gurus. Just as we would expect our doctor or attorney (or financial advisor) to obtain and maintain a certain level of education, we should expect our trainer to do the same. Whether an exercise science degree or certification, some of the most respected training certifications come from: The American Council on Exercise (ACE), The National Academy of Sports Medicine (NASM), and International Sports Sciences Association (ISSA).[5] These organizations assure that our trainer has at least a basic level of fitness knowledge and understanding of the human anatomy and physiology, and that they keep abreast of current changes and thinking. A certification from any of these respected associations also assures that our trainer understands that fitness does not just happen on the bench press; diet and the bigger nutrition, rest and sleep, and stress levels all play important roles in maintaining a healthy lifestyle.

Just as with our money, the personality of our trainer is also a key consideration. Some trainers are, by nature, softer and willing to compromise on workouts. Others are demanding drill sergeants who will push us to the verge of exhaustion. We should select a trainer that fits with our personality and pushes our muscles just a bit out of our comfort zone.

Think of our workout like this: people don't train to run a 26.2-mile marathon by running short sprints around the track or even by running a total of 10.0 miles in a week. If they did, then both physically and mentally, they wouldn't have the energy or mental stamina to push much further than the 10 miles their body is comfortable with. To train for a marathon, we need to push beyond our goal, so that our minds and bodies will be comfortable in reaching the finish line consistently.

When selecting either professional, make sure you have really looked at the professional's qualifications.

Chapter 3 Easy Learning concepts:

3. *Fiscal – Seek an Advisor that shares your philosophy and is willing to work with you as a fiduciary, regardless of fancy-sounding designations.*
3. *Physical – Find a Certified Personal Trainer who has expertise with your specific needs and is compatible with your personality.*

Chapter 4

Starting Early: Pay It Now or Pay It Later

As we saw in our two friends example with Fred and Barney in Chapter 2, starting early allows us to take advantage of what Albert Einstein may have once described as the strongest force in the universe: **COMPOUND INTEREST**.[1] Our money grows, the interest gets added, and our money grows again. Do this long enough and a relatively small pile of money eventually becomes quite large.

Because Einstein was a physicist, he wasn't content to come up with a pretty cool metaphysical law of nature in plain English, he had to get all complicated and derive a mathematical formula with numbers and letters. Fortunately for us, the formula turned out pretty easy and is known as the "Rule of 72."[2] NB: There is no proof that Einstein came up with the "Rule of 72," although it is often attributed to him. Most likely, it was developed 400 years earlier by an Italian

Friar (and coworker to Leonardo DaVinci) named Luca Pacioli in 1494.

It states that when we divide the number 72 by the number of years we are willing to wait on an investment, the result will be what interest rate we need to achieve in order to double our money. If I am only willing to wait 9 years for my investment, then 72 divided by 9 years equals a required 8.0% average return to double my money.

But the reality is that few of us only want to double our $6,000 investment and fewer still start at 22 years old. At starting salary wages, saving $500 a month is a daunting task bordering on the edge of impossible. Therefore, let's look at some more realistic scenarios. To do that, we will need to pick more reasonable inputs: the amount of money we can truly put aside, and the return that we can truly achieve.

How much can we save?

In the fourth quarter of 2019, the average American salary was $48,672 a year.[3] We know that Uncle Sam is going to take some off the top (according to the IRS, the average American paid 11.4% in 2017)[4] but here let's assume 10.0% or $4,867 for easier calculations. We also know that many states also apply income tax (albeit at a smaller rate), so let's assume 2.0%[5] or $973, leaving us with only $42,831 a year or $3,569 a month.

From that we will need to take out costs for housing, food, transportation, and health care.

Depending on where you live in the United States, that likely consumes nearly all of that $3,569 a month, if not even more.[6] Realistically, when we add in costs for clothing, entertainment, insurance, and utilities, the average American is operating in the negative, meaning we aren't investing, we are using credit cards and other forms of debt just to get by.

Admittedly, a spouse or partner adding their salary to the household helps the economics, but often adding a spouse or partner (which is a positive) generally results in eventually adding a child (which is an additional significant cost) or two. Even the addition of four-legged children adds costs, with the average American spending almost $500 a year.[7]

In fact, the average American saved just 7.5% of their **NET INCOME** (their income after taxes) in 2019.[8] On our $42,831 above, that comes out to just $3,212 or $267 per month.

What are reasonable returns?

Since January 1st, 2000 through the end of 2019, the **DOW JONES INDUSTRIAL AVERAGE (DJIA)**, has on average increased 5.8%.[9] If (and this is a wholly unreasonable if) we completely ignored the year 2008, what was formerly known as the Great Recession, the DJIA returned 7.9% on average. Reality is that we will experience ups and downs in the stock market, experience good years and bad, so using 5.8% is the realistic assumption.

Some clients prefer to benchmark themselves against the somewhat more technology-heavy **STANDARD AND POORS 500 (S&P500)**. Over the same period, the S&P500 averaged a very similar 5.6%.[10]

A quick note about "Average Returns": They work a lot better over longer periods of time than shorter ones. For example, let's say we invest $100 in the stock market on January 1st. The market has a horrible year and loses 50.0%. On December 31st our portfolio value will be only $50. Now let's say the next year we have a great year, and the stock market gains 50.0%. Our portfolio value on December 31st of the second year will only be $75...not $100...and our average return is 0.0%.

This works because the first year 50.0% of the starting value ($100) is $50. But in year two, 50.0% of the starting value ($50) is only $25, taking us back to $75. We realize the math is pretty simple, but you would be surprised by the number of people who make that simple math mistake. In order to get back to the $100 we started with on January 1st of the first year, our second-year returns would need to be 100.0%...and our average return over the period would be 25.0%.

Now that we have realistic assumptions, let's revisit Barney's outcome. We remember he starts investing at 32 and now we see he puts $267 a month away at an average return of 5.8%. At 65 years old, Barney has put away $108,000 of his own money and compound interest has grown the portfolio to

$339,000, significantly less than his 1 million dollar jackpot in our last example.

Let's assume Barney starts a family, buys a house, and sends his kids off to college, and doesn't start saving for his retirement until age 45. He will save $64,000 of his own money and compound interest will grow the value to $122,000.

Any number of factors will go into your own retirement projections. How much can we save? How long can we save for? Do opportunities allow us to increase our savings or do circumstances force us to reduce them? What level of risk are we willing to accept? And what levels of return do we want to achieve?

Just as we try to add to our portfolio, many of us try to subtract from our waist. Remember our Physical Fitness Rule 1? To lose weight we need to burn more calories than we consume. Fortunately, in weight loss there is another pretty easy formula to remember as well. A pound of fat equals about 3,500 **CALORIES,** a unit of energy given off by a specific amount of food. This means that if we want to lose 1 pound of fat, we need to strip 3,500 calories out of our diet OR burn an extra 3,500 calories in our exercise.

Let's put that one in perspective as well. The National Institute of Health recommends an average American consume between 2,000 and 2,500 calories a day for healthy living.[11] The reality is we are consuming about 3,600 a day today, or 25,200 calories per week.[12]

To lose 10 lbs in a week (we SERIOUSLY DO NOT RECOMMEND you try to lose 10 lbs in a week), we need to take 35,000 calories out of that. Since we only have 25,200 calories from the food we eat, we cannot consume anything but water, AND we still need to get another 10,000 calories from exercise. For a 180 lb person, walking a mile burns roughly 100 calories; to knock out those last 10,000 calories, we will need to walk 100 miles...on an empty stomach.

A much easier idea is to not put on the extra pounds in the first place. Eating healthier, smaller portions of more nutritious food and a light to moderate exercise regimen from the start will keep us feeling leaner and healthier, instead of having to go on a starvation diet later to shed the pounds.

Whether it's starting earlier on investing or getting back into the summer beach body shape, time is one of our greatest allies. Little incremental steps, taken over a longer period of time, are easier to accomplish and return greater results.

Chapter 4 Easy Learning concepts:

4. *Fiscal – The Rule of 72 helps us find the time and rate we need to double our money.*
4. *Physical – 3,500 calories are equal to one pound of fat. We need to 'cut' or 'burn' those calories to lose weight.*

CHAPTER 5

Getting Started

By now, hopefully, we are grasping the importance of not letting our investment portfolio or fitness goals drive us, but for us to drive our investment and fitness goals. That in itself is an extremely important, nay critical mindset that we need to adopt for success. If we allow our fears, other people's opinions, or life itself to chart our course, we will always be at the mercy of the ebbs and flows of the universe.

You are probably saying to yourself at this point, "Okay, you've got me convinced. Now what?" First, we need to understand that there are only 3 things we can do with money: hold it as **CASH** (the paper green stuff that comes out of the ATM), lend it to someone, or buy something with it. Yes, we concede that you can give it away, but the point of this book is to improve our financial (and physical) situation... so let us revise that to there are only 3 things we can do to grow our money.

"Cash is King!" A trite saying that everyone has heard, but there is a great deal of truth to it. We need cash to pay the mortgage or rent. We need cash to buy food to eat. We need cash to fill our cars with gas to get us to our job, so we can trade hours of work for... more cash.

Offset that truth with the very real fact that holding onto cash has its own set of problems that we will go into deeper in the next chapter. But for now, let us agree to set our working rule of thumb to be: everyone needs to have 6 to 9 months of average monthly expenses in cash on hand. We should also agree that holding cash doesn't really help us grow our investment portfolio. With most banks offering less than 1.0% interest on a checking or savings account, and many offering 0.0% – with fees for ATM usage – writing too many checks or monthly service charges, a bank account may actually cost us more than we gain.[1]

Second, we can lend our money to someone, some corporation, or even some state or country. You'll learn over the next 2 chapters that cutting the bank out of the middle of our relationship can increase our return on our investments AND decrease the taxes we owe. Unlike loaning money to your crazy Uncle Eddie (that is a gamble as to whether he will ever pay you back), these loans are complex legal contracts, some of which can and do legitimately offer guarantees of low or no risk. Just because the actual contract itself is complex doesn't mean the underlying principles are impossible to understand. In Chapter 6, we will explain the difference between the many types of

Getting Started

BONDS and show you how they add a very important income stream to our diversified portfolio.

Finally, we can buy something. For the purposes of this book, we are specifically referring to stocks (**or EQUITIES**) but many of the same principles apply to owning real estate, investment art, or pork belly futures. There are a number of 'watch outs' in the Stock Market, and in Chapter 6 we will go deeper into many of those and how to make stock selections that meet both our **RISK TOLERANCE,** an abstract measurement of how much risk we can handle before panicking, and investment return needs. In Chapters 7, 8, and 9, we will cover some of the more advanced investments, including real estate and futures, but for now content ourselves with the idea that we can buy something that will work for us, even while we are sleeping.

If you haven't already guessed, the similarities between the world of health and fitness and the world of finances are surprising. As we alluded to earlier, fitness likewise really only has three types of activities. We have strength training, which builds power and to a lesser extent speed, we have cardio training, which builds endurance, and we have flexibility training, which improves our range of motion and can refine some of our balance and fine motor skills. We will delve deeper into each of these three components of fitness in the coming chapters.

But for now, recognize that strength training is like cash: the foundation or core of a healthy fitness portfolio. Everyone needs it to some lesser or greater extent depending on our objectives.

Endurance training turns the muscles developed in strength training into effective tools. Once we have achieved a basic level of physical strength, we need to be able to apply the muscles for our benefit. The longer we can apply them, the further we can use them. The more consistently we repeat the motions, the more we increase the return we get from them. Here, we would compare endurance training to stocks, bonds, and mutual funds.

And finally, flexibility training means refining the strength and endurance to accomplish a specific goal with predictable regularity. In sports lore, it is believed that Kobe Bryant refused to leave practice before he made 400 shots, and he would practice making those shots in a darkened gym so he could not see the basket. Further, he would also practice the same shot over and over for hours on end. Not because he wasn't a good shooter, but because he wanted to really refine his touch, how much strength was required to push the ball towards the hoop, to get the 'feel' as it were. And because of that relentless, disciplined attention to his fine motor skills, he became a clutch shooter with some of the highest offensive percentages of all time.[2] And similarly, in the Fiscal world, there are additional investments that can take a strong portfolio to the next level. But to continue the basketball metaphor, for now we are working on layups, we will shoot three-pointers later.

Our takeaway here is that saving and investing doesn't have to be scary, or even require a Ph.D. in advanced statistical analysis. Sure, there are many jobs within the finance field that do get very esoteric very quickly, but those skills are well beyond what we need to understand and build our own portfolio that will get us where we want to be.

Chapter 5 Easy Learning concepts:

5. *Fiscal – There are only 3 things we can do with our money to make it grow: hold as cash, lend, or buy.*
5. *Physical – There are really only 3 types of activities that we can do to improve our health: strength, endurance, and flexibility.*

CHAPTER **6**

Beginner Level

Don't let the physical form of cash fool you. Paper checks and plastic credit cards are cash. Gold **BULLION** (coins or bars) or **BITCOINS** are NOT cash. The distinguishing factor between them is one can be traded today at a value that everyone knows, understands, and accepts. The other (despite the name) takes time to convert into a medium that everyone else can work with. Think of it this way: if we go to the supermarket for a loaf of bread, the cashier is not likely to know the value of an 18th century Spanish Doubloon or what .0000145 Bitcoins is worth. That cashier won't trade us the loaf of bread for either of those "currencies." That same cashier will trade us a loaf of bread for a $5 bill or the swipe of our credit card.

Because life happens, we need to have cash on hand. The general rule of thumb is before we invest our first dollar, we need to have between 6 and 9 months of cash available at all times. This is often called the "emergency fund" or the "rainy day fund" and it is where we go when an illness keeps us out of work or the car needs new tires or the dreaded check engine light leaves us stranded on the side of the road. We can immediately go to the emergency fund and cover the costs. We don't have to worry about whether our investments are trading at highs or lows. We don't need to go through the process of liquidating or converting our assets back to the exchangeable green stuff. Bam! It's there, we have it, we pay it, we move on.

Cash generally should not be stored under our mattress (literally), although people who live in areas prone to natural disasters may want to think about it. In the event that the electricity goes out, those ATM machines aren't going to work, so having SOME cash at home and on hand isn't a horrible idea. For the rest of us, cash should be stored at our local bank or credit union. Why? Because of a little thing called FDIC (Federal Depositors Insurance Corporation) insurance. FDIC insurance is the US Government's solemn promise to us that if the bank burns down, if it is robbed, or if it goes out of business, the Government will step in and replace our money – protections that the Government doesn't offer to the cash under our bed.[1]

Having cash is key. For us to put our money in an account at the bank, the bank (or credit union) will likely give us a small token reward. That is called interest and is a percentage of our total deposit that the bank pays us for our loyalty. In a savings or checking account, that reward is often very small (today some banks don't even offer interest on checking or savings accounts) because the bank doesn't know when we are going to come in and ask for our money back. The bank has to balance the money they loan out, with the risk that we are going to ask for ours back every single day. If we are willing to commit to the bank that we won't take our money out for a set period of time (say 6 months or 1 year) that contract is known as a **CERTIFICATE OF DEPOSIT or CD**. Because the bank knows that we won't be back tomorrow for our money, they can use it for longer periods of time before having to worry that we will take our money out.

While we know that an FDIC insured bank is safer than under our mattress, there are two glaring problems with that arrangement. First, any interest that the bank pays us that is less than the inflation rate cuts into our **PURCHASING POWER** *[see below]*. The second is that the bank is using our money to make them money, and they keep the largest portion of the profits for themselves. Oh yeah, just to add insult to injury, the Government also turns around and taxes us on our portion, making our ultimate return on investment even smaller.

What exactly is the loss of purchasing power? We know from previous chapters that inflation in the United States runs around 3.9%. That means a loaf of bread that costs $1.00 today will likely cost $1.03 next year. If the bank only pays us 1.0% on our deposit,

$1.00 left in the bank for that year will earn $0.01 interest and our total at the end of the year will only be $1.01. Last year we could afford the loaf of bread, next year we are 2 pennies short. Over time, that difference can seriously set us back.

Think of it another way. 30 years ago, we went to the gas station in a pair of comfy jeans. In our left pocket we had a $20 bill. In our right pocket we had another $20 bill. With the $20 in our left pocket, we filled up our car with gas, went inside, and bought a pack of cigarettes and a bottle of soda. We went home that night and threw the jeans in the washing machine where they sat for 30 years. Today, we take those jeans out of the washer, put them on, and go to the gas station. We reach into our right pocket and find that second $20 bill. It's unlikely we will be able to even fill up our car with the money. It's still $20, but it buys less today than the same amount did 30 years ago. That is the loss of purchasing power. Money we leave in the bank is still our money, and it probably is still growing, but when we take it out, it buys less than it did before.

There is a second problem with banks holding onto our money. What do we think they do with it? Wrap it up in nice neat bundles and put it in the safe waiting for us to come back and claim it? We would be wrong! Banks take our money and give it to customers looking for loans. Those customers pay the bank back (with interest) and the bank quietly slides the money back into the safe for us to come in and collect it, none the wiser. If we play this scenario out with a customer who asks to borrow money for buying a house (a mortgage), he will likely pay the bank 4.0% interest on his loan – and be happy about it. But if the bank only pays us 1.0% interest...where did the other 3.0% of interest go? That's right, to the bank. *We* took the risk that our money would get lost or destroyed, but *the bank* made 3 times the return that we did. And just for fun, Uncle Sam is going to make sure he takes taxes out of our share.

While a foundational building block to our finances is cash, one of the most basic building blocks to healthy living is daily exercise. At the bare minimum, exercise lubricates our joints and allows us to maintain a quality of movement. Our bodies adapt to any repeated activity. If we sit too long, the muscles contract and our joints tighten. Then when we stand up, it takes more energy to start a body in motion than it does to keep it moving. As one of our trainers used to say, "Motion is lotion."

We don't need a lot of expensive equipment or complicated weight machines to get started. In fact, we have seen many people come into the gym and jump on a piece of equipment without understanding how it works, use the equipment wrong, and hurt themselves. Take a stair climber for example. The stair climber is an evolution (or the next level up) of a treadmill. On a treadmill, we work our glutes, quads, hamstrings, and hip flexors to maintain a largely flat, steady, forward motion. It is great exercise to build cardiovascular endurance. A stair climber refocuses those same muscles in a slightly different direction. Our legs have to lift higher to clear the height of the next stair, and there is more power required from our glutes to thrust our weight forward and propel us upwards instead of along a flat path. Intermixing our workout between the two machines creates an intermediate level workout.

Starting our exercise routine on a stair master can be a mistake. We would be asking our muscles to immediately jump from a sedentary state to a high-intensity state and damage, pain, and injury will likely result. A weekly routine of walking and stretching with a couple of sessions that incorporate light resistance training will lay the groundwork for a lifetime of healthy habits.

Chapter 6 Easy Learning concepts:

6. *Fiscal – Cash is King, but no more than 6 to 9 months in an emergency fund.*
6. *Physical – Establish a daily routine that focuses on form and technique.*

CHAPTER **7**

Intermediate Level

If you are shaking your head wondering why you never thought long and hard about banks taking advantage of your deposits, don't worry, most people haven't.

But where to put the rest of our savings? How do we get in on that bank gig and start earning that higher interest for ourselves? There is a simple way to do just that – loan our money, cut the bank out of the middle, and keep all the profit for ourselves. It's called a bond.

A bond is simply a contract between us and a borrower where we give over a pile of money for a specific period of time. The borrower will pay us interest, and at the end of that period of time, will return our pile of money. It may not be the exact same $100 bill we gave the borrower at the beginning, but as long as the borrower returns a legal $100 bill – do we really care?

The astute among us will notice that when we took our money out of the bank and signed this contract with the borrower, we gave up our FDIC insurance protection. You, astute reader, are ahead of the curve in recognizing the increased risk that the borrower may **DEFAULT**. But what if we loaned our money to the exact same government that issues the FDIC insurance that makes us feel better about the safety of the bank? That's right! We can loan our money to the US Government. We have a contract for a period of time. We give the Government a pile of cash, the Government pays us interest, and at the end of the contract the Government gives us our pile of cash back. If we loan our money for up to 1 year, it's called a *Treasury Note (T-NOTE)*...up to 2 years to 10 years is called a *T-BILL*, and for longer than 10 years it's called a *T-BOND*. The only difference is the length of time we are contracted for.

Now as to that risk. A Treasury investment is the only investment legally allowed to be called **RISK-FREE**. Make a note of that. When we see an advertisement for a Risk-Free/No Risk/Guaranteed Investment, the advertiser better be referring to a Treasury Investment or something shady is being pulled over our eyes. Why, we ask, is a Treasury Investment risk-free? Simply because the US Government controls the mint. If the Government doesn't happen to have a pile of money to give back to us when the contract is up... it turns on the printing presses and cranks out a couple of new $100 bills. The US Government is the only organization that can legally print money for us.

Intermediate Level

As an added bonus, the Government, as a way of saying thank you for loaning them money, won't tax the interest they pay us. Already, we have cut out the bank and captured all the interest return, we loaned it to the same organization that runs FDIC Insurance, and we saved on taxes. Sadly though, no good thing comes without an ugly side, and because this is such a great deal, here the ugly side is that the interest the Government is willing to give us is often very low. In fact, some countries like Japan and Germany actually charge us **NEGATIVE INTEREST**[1] to put our money with them. Historically, 10-year US Treasury Investments have returned around 4.0%.[2]

If we are willing to take on a little more risk, then we might consider municipal bonds. **MUNICIPAL BONDS** (also known as Munis) are bonds (contracts) with local, regional, and state governments. They work the same way Treasury Bonds work (even the bonus of Uncle Sam not collecting his share) but don't carry that risk-free guarantee. Technically, states cannot print money (thus the distinction), however, state governments can levy taxes, whether through property, sales, or income tax, to give us back our pile of money at the end of the contract. Because we give up the risk-free guarantee, Munis pay slightly higher returns, averaging 5.26% over the last 20 years.[3]

If we are willing to take on even more risk, large corporations are often looking to borrow money. We would think that Apple, Coca-Cola, and IBM would have piles of money laying around or could easily borrow from the banks on the strength of their name alone. And we are probably correct, but the reasons a corporation may want to borrow from us versus a bank are complex and varied, which we will talk about a little more in the next chapter. Unfortunately, because corporations can neither print money nor impose taxes, the risk level of lending to them is higher. This combined with the fact that Uncle Sam doesn't give us any thank you on our interest means that the return in large corporation investment-grade debt is also higher, ranging between 3.0% and 15.0% historically.[4]

More risk? Smaller companies. We take even more chance that the borrower won't be able to repay the loan, and as such we demand higher compensation for our troubles.

Even *more* risk? **FOREIGN SOVEREIGN DEBT.** There are over 192 countries out there that need to borrow US dollars to pay for goods and services. Countries like Germany probably won't go out of business anytime soon. Countries like Argentina however have defaulted 9 times on its foreign debt between 1827 and 2020.[5] We should be compensated more for the more risk we take.

Ready to see more results in the fitness world, too? Once our muscles have grown accustomed to moving, it's time to start pushing the muscles beyond their comfort zone and introduce weights. Adding weights (please start small and increase over time as your ability allows) to your exercise begins to incorporate concepts of balance, endurance, and obviously strength. Adding weights introduces the "overload" principle.

Right now, we want to try a simple exercise. We want to place a higher demand on our bodies than we are used to during the normal business day. Stand up and place both feet flat on the ground next to our desk. Our feet should be shoulder-width apart. Sit our butts down like we are sitting on a chair and then stand back up. Now find something that weighs 10-25 lbs and repeat this exercise. For most people, this will be harder due to the added weight. This is the overload concept. By training with the extra weight, the muscles are forced to adapt and build themselves stronger. In the future when we perform the squat without weight, it will become easier due to these exercises.

In this simple example, we have gone from a relatively basic, single, dimensional, flat exertion of our muscles to a more complex multi-dimensional exertion. This exercise put different and increased stresses on the muscles in a controlled fashion.

In fitness, once multiple muscle activation has begun, the increase in calorie burn increases exponentially. Just like you in investing: one single investment may help you grow your money, but adding diversification and multiple investments can help your portfolio take off.

Chapter 7 Easy Learning concepts:

7. *Fiscal – We can lend our money in a contract called a Bond.*
7. *Physical – Progressively incorporating more complex exercises raises the return on our physical investment.*

CHAPTER **8**

Advanced Level

So far, we have covered two of the three things that we can do to build our investment portfolio. To re-cap, the easiest and most basic thing to do is to hold it as cash. The more intermediate level option is to lend the cash to someone else. The hardest option (and more advanced level) is to buy something, and here we mean specifically **MUTUAL FUNDS, EXCHANGE TRADED FUNDS (ETFs)**, and individual equities. We will cover buying other "expert investments" such as real estate, options, futures, and bitcoin in later chapters – so for now, let's just focus on these advanced products.

First, we need to understand exactly what a stock is. Originally, a stock was a piece of paper, a contract, or maybe more accurately, a receipt reflecting our ownership. The first known stock certificate looks like a children's note scribbled on a scrap of a brown paper bag. It represented an ownership right in a Dutch East India Company from 1606.[1] At the time, the Dutch East India Company was the biggest and most powerful company in the world. Today, most stocks are held electronically as 1s and 0s in a big computer 'cloud' in the sky, but they still reflect our ownership rights. Generally, the ownership right that we are most interested in is the right to the profits at the end of the day.

In a simplistic world, a company would issue 100 shares of stock. Each share would entitle the owner of that share to exactly $1/100^{th}$ of the company. $1/100^{th}$ of the assets. $1/100^{th}$ of the profits. We could buy more shares and collectively own a bigger percentage of the company. Think about it...if Apple had only issued 100 shares of stock...and we owned 1 share or 1.0%... and in 2019 Apple made $55.6 billion in net income, then we would be entitled to $556 million.

In real life, companies have many more shares of stock than just 100. Most large companies have billions of shares and even smaller companies have millions. The reasons for this are many and too complex for this book, but suffice it to say, the share of stock we own probably represents less than 1.0% of a company, but it still entitles us to our proportional share of the bounty at the end of the year.[2]

Mutual Funds and ETFs
If we only had $1.00 to invest in the stock market, where would we put it? As of today's writing, there

are over 65,000 individual publicly traded companies available to the American investor. If this is our first time to the pool, diving into the deep end is a scary prospect. Wouldn't it be great if we could buy a percentage of a couple of different companies with that same $1.00 and spread our chances of picking a winner? Mutual Funds and ETFs allow us to do that.

With a Mutual Fund or ETF, we are not buying an individual company's stock, but a bucket of stocks that a professional manager manages (Mutual Funds) or a computer algorithm follows (ETFs). We own a percentage of the bucket. Subtle differences in the actual mix, methodology, and personalities involved drive differences in performance. Managers of mutual funds tend to move a little quicker because there is a real live person managing the investments in real-time, but that human may pick right or wrong. Computer algorithms move slower because they react to the market's ups and DOWNS. As a computer though, ETFs don't have a person to apply knowledge, experience, or gut feelings, they react indiscriminately.[3]

In addition to different financial companies selling similar buckets, there is a similarity between ETF and Mutual Fund buckets as well. You can buy broad market-based buckets or sector-specific buckets depending on your interest. The following chart shows how some ETFs and Mutual Funds can share the same space.

ETF	Mutual Fund
QQQ Tracks the S&P500 performance	AIVSX comprises top 150 US companies
NOBL Tracks good dividend payers	FRDPX comprises rising dividend companies
XAR Tracks the Aerospace Industry	FSDAX is made of Select Defense & Aerospace

Ultimately, buying a bucket as opposed to an individual stock gives us a wider spread of our money. Some stocks in the bucket will perform worse than others, but the theory is more stocks will do well and the bucket overall will make positive returns.

Individual Stocks

Whereas investing in a mutual fund or ETF is like shooting a shotgun, investing in individual stocks is like using a revolver. We must be a lot more accurate in our aim and shooting.

There are two types of stock that we care about. Having said that, MorningStar (the company that assigns values [stars] to a stock based on its analysis and evaluation of the strength of the company) breaks stocks down into 9 types, and many people toss around terms like small cap growth, large cap blend, or mid-cap value – so let us quickly address the complexities in the naming convention before we get into the two types of stock and what the differences mean for our investment portfolio.

Advanced Level

Companies come in three sizes: Small, Medium, and Large. Here, experts will argue there are Mega companies and Micro companies. There are domestic, foreign, emerging market, BRIC, and Asian companies, and those nuances are important, but we can quickly get lost in the weeds if we don't keep the discussion at a certain higher level. For our purposes, there are only three sizes of companies and it doesn't really matter where the company is located.

Small Cap (Small Capitalization) companies are companies with a market value of less than $500 million. Mid-Cap (Medium Capitalization) companies have a market value between $501 million and $1 billion, and as we can guess, Large Cap (Large Capitalization) companies have a market value of over $1 billion. Market valuation is simply the total number of shares of stock a company has issued times the price the stock is trading at. Following us so far? Good!

Now, those same three size categories can be broken into 3 more segments based on what type of corporate vision the company is following. A vision that says the company is going to focus on growth through spending in research, advertising, and maybe acquiring competitors or market share at all costs is considered a Growth company, and many newer or technology-based companies have this focus. A company whose vision is slow, steady, consistent maintenance of high-quality and protection of the brand and spends their money appropriately is known as a Value company and are found predominately among the more mature companies. A Blend company is somewhere between Growth and Value and generally means that the company's vision is to continue to get bigger, but it is not willing to do so at the detriment of everything else.

Thus, we can have small companies focused on getting bigger (Small Cap Growth) and we can have big companies focused on delivering quality, consistent performance (Large Cap Value). The companies in the middle who split their focus, we are going to dump into the Blend category. 3 sizes by 3 types gives us the 9 categories that MorningStar refers to.[4]

To build a better portfolio, we are going to want to own some combination of Growth stocks and Value stocks. We want to own Growth stocks because when a growth company performs well, their share price/stock price goes up. Companies like Apple have grown from $10 a share to over $300. Some stocks have even split and grown back over $300. When we buy stock in a Growth company, that is exactly what we hope will happen. We want to buy the stock at a low price, hold it while it grows, and then sell it at a high price. Returns in the Growth stock universe average close to 13.6% on an annual basis.[5]

We own Value stocks because we want to harvest our share of the company's profits along our investing journey. Those profit harvests (known as dividends) allow us to use the money as income to supplement our salary or social security, or maybe to collect them into a little pile that we ultimately use to buy some more stock. The point is that Value companies pay dividends, and dividends create cash. And what did we say about cash? Exactly right! Besides it being King, there are three things we can do with it. A little bonus to Value stocks is their price can go up as well. A company that has a consistent track record of paying good dividends can see its price increase to the point that we get to sell it at a higher value than we bought it. A double benefit! In the Value stock universe, returns have averaged approximately 7.0% since 2000.[6]

If you've made it to this point in the chapter and are still following along, congratulations. The differences between the size of the company, the company's philosophy, and the company's performance are what make owning stock an advanced skill. Remember what we said in Chapter 2, we are not alone in managing our portfolio, a skilled, trustworthy Financial Advisor can coach us through the process.

Volatility and Pricing

We are going to push on and broach the two biggest "watch-outs" for buying/owning/selling stock. The first concept is volatility. We all know that stock markets go up and they go down. It follows then that the price of actual individual stocks goes up and down as well. The size of that swing from up to down to up is volatility. A stock price that normally trades between $30 and $40 per share would be considered relatively stable or to have low volatility. A stock price that has traded between $75 and $202 per share during the last 52 weeks is considered to be highly volatile.

While the subject of market volatility could make up a book in and of itself, we are well-armed if we only know that volatility is tracked on a chart known as the VIX. Normal VIX volatility measures between 15 and 20. In late March 2020, the VIX shot up to over 80 as investors fled the stock market after the official designation of the COVID-19 illness a Pandemic.[7]

The second watch-out concept is the stock price itself. What makes up a fair price? An over-valued or under-valued price? Traditionally, price is a function of what our expectations are about the future performance of the company. We are paying today for an ownership right to the value the company is expected to create tomorrow.

The **PRICE TO EARNINGS RATIO** is one of the most common measures of a stock price. The P/E ratio represents the company's earnings over the last twelve months times a factor (which is different for each sector in the market – generally 15) and determines a fair market price. Buying low P/Es and selling when they are high makes money and, when we carefully watch the company's operating

Advanced Level

performance, can help us determine where the stock price will go up or down.[8]

- P/E in Oil and Gas (Integrated) – roughly 12.7x
- P/E in Wireless Cell Phones – roughly 27.2x

Here it should be noted that the reasons for a stock's price to go up or down are many. Generally, the underlying performance of the company drives a significant portion: as in, did the company's sales increase from one year to the next? Did they make more profit than last year? All might drive a stock price higher or lower depending on the answer. Another piece of what drives the share price is consumer sentiment. Brands that sign on pro-athletes may experience huge upticks if the athlete does well. Brands that experience public relations disasters (remember BP and the Deep Water Horizon in the Gulf of Mexico) can watch their price sink – pun intended. And then there are times like 2020, when the world just turns off for a few months, that all stock prices go down, regardless of the underlying performance and even absent any specific bad press.

When a good investor hears a buddy on the golf course talk about the next sure thing that a friend of their friend told them, the wise investor thinks about all of these factors. The bad investor just throws money at the chance like a lottery ticket. When selecting which stock to purchase, we should expect our Financial Advisor to combine all of these factors into their recommendations:

- How much return do we need to accomplish our goals? – that may lean the recommendation towards a Growth or Value stock
- How much volatility can we, the investor, bear? – watching our portfolio value swing wildly day to day is tough
- How is the company doing performance-wise? – how do they make money and what do the public relations look like?
- How are the sector and the overall market performing? – are we mid-Market Crisis, or booming in an unprecedented period of stable growth?

Congratulations! We've moved past the intermediate level of our workout routine. We are feeling great, looking great, and are now ready for a new challenge. Let's incorporate the more advanced principles of fitness: the 6 skill-related components of agility, balance, coordination, speed, power, and reaction time. We should continue to work on the exercises that we have developed so far, but to advance our trainer may ask us to perform the exercise on an unstable surface like a balance pad to promote more activation in our leg muscles and integrate our core. These new approaches to familiar exercises continue

Advanced Level

to keep overloading the muscles and help them adapt to additional demands.

We want to revisit the squat exercise we did in the previous chapter. Now, pick up that same 10-25 lb weight, hold it in one hand, and perform the exercise again. Notice your body shift from side to side, and maintaining even balance becomes harder. Whereas in the last chapter we were simply loading muscles by adding weight, now by offsetting the weight we have incorporated balance and coordination to 'overload' the muscles and engage our core. We should feel our muscles react to the uneven load on the body and we should feel our center of gravity readjusting itself to compensate for the unequal loading. Did we feel our stomach muscles tighten as the body centered itself? If not, repeat the exercise one more time while focusing on tightening our abdominal muscles. This exercise incorporates both balance and strength.

Holding a weight in one arm while performing the squat seems advanced in terms of fitness, but it is very applicable to the person reaching to grab an item off the top shelf of a closet who needs to maintain their balance. In our active aging class, we also work on speed and agility because the only place we see people fall in slow motion is in the movies. When we trip and fall, we fall fast and hard, this is why reaction time is important. When the brain is trained to react quickly using speed and agility, it will move the body into position to prevent or minimize injury.

In these simple examples, we have gone from a relatively basic, single-dimensional, flat exertion of our muscles to a more complex, multi-dimensional exertion. Our leg muscles didn't just push us straight up, we engaged multiple muscles to keep us balanced side to side.

Chapter 8 Easy Learning concepts:

8. *Fiscal – Buying a stock is a complicated decision not to be contemplated simply because a buddy recommended it, but mutual funds and ETFs can help spread the risk of picking losers.*
8. *Physical – We need to increase dynamic demands on our muscles to continue seeing results.*

Chapter 9

Expert Level

For the expert investor options, futures, hedge funds, and derivatives are additional ways to capture gains when the market is moving up and even when the market is moving down. To the novice, these investments are little better than "playing" the stock market in that if we don't know exactly what we are doing with these complex instruments, we are really just gambling. For the average reader of this book, we don't want to provide too much information because human curiosity will inspire us to go out and try something that, if not carefully supervised, will likely hurt us. We are going to keep this chapter at a super high level, enough to make us familiar with the concepts, but not educated enough to get hurt.

Options
We don't need to actually sell stock from our portfolio to make money. We can make money by borrowing shares to sell at a high price (buy a **PUT**) or by letting

someone else borrow our shares to sell at a high price (selling a put). In both cases, whoever does the borrowing will ultimately need to replace the shares.

For example: if we think the stock of XYZ company is at an all-time high today of $100 and we feel sure the price is going to go down... we can borrow 100 shares of XYZ stock from someone and sell it at the $100 price. When the price goes down (say to $90), we can buy the 100 shares back from the open market and give them back to the person who loaned us their shares. Of course, we'll pay that person something to borrow the shares, but we make the profit between the $100 sales price and $90 replacement price.

BEWARE: if the price doesn't go down to $90, but actually goes up to $105 we still have to buy those 100 shares in the open market and give them back to the lender at the contracted time, so we may actually lose money!

Conversely, we can make money with an options **CALL**. If we buy a call, we buy the right to purchase someone else's shares at a lower price, and if we sell a call we agree to sell someone else those shares at the lower price.

For example: if we think the price of XYZ is really low today at $50 and we feel sure the market is going to go up, we can buy a call from some other person in the market which entitles us to buy their shares for $50. When the market does go up, say to $90, we exercise the call, purchase the shares from the lender at $50, and turn around and sell them in the market at $90, making $40 a share (less than what we paid the lender for the right).

NOTE: unlike a put, if the price never goes over the $50 price that we agreed on, we wouldn't exercise the call and we would only lose the money we paid the lender for the right to buy those shares.

If we want to get even more exotic, we can buy both a put and a call at the same time (called a **STRADDLE**) to limit our losses and maximize our gains.

Futures

A future is comparable to an option, in that we are buying something based on our expectations on what is going to happen in the future. If, for example, we feel strongly that the coming winter will be exceptionally harsh, and that will impact the orange trees in Florida, making the price of oranges more expensive and lessen the availability of orange juice, we may choose to lock in the price of oranges with a futures contract today. We would lock in with an orange farmer on a price today, and the farmer would deliver the oranges on the date of the contract.

In April of 2020, we saw one sector of the futures market almost implode because beginners were playing around in a space they didn't fully understand. The price of oil had been moving wildly for a couple of months proceeding, so people were buying oil futures based on their guess of where the price was going to be in May. Then the Coronavirus pandemic struck, almost bringing the oil industry to a halt. That left a lot of oil in storage tanks and on floating oil tankers headed to port. At the same time, customers who had purchased oil futures for delivery in May had the increasingly difficult task of trying to find places to put the oil they had contracted for. For a period of 3 days, the price of May contracts actually went negative, meaning people with May Oil Futures were paying us to take their contract because they had no place to put the oil they were due.[1]

Hedge Funds and Derivatives

Both hedge funds and derivatives are so complicated that there are many thick books dedicated to either subject on their own. Both are generally considered very risky and in many cases to even buy one/into one, you are required to sign lots of legal paperwork acknowledging that you recognize that you could lose all your money. We don't know about you, but going into an investment where we have to legally acknowledge that we might lose everything from the outset doesn't inspire confidence. That being said, let us quickly learn what they are.

Hedge funds are very small, closed, high-risk mutual funds on steroids. Small, not in the sense of the amount invested – some are huge, with over $1 billion – but in the sense that hedge funds limit the participation to a smaller number of people than just being open to the general public. Closed because of the legal documentation discussed above and the qualifications, assets, and experience needed to even get a look at the documentation. Risky because they are investing in non-traditional ways of making money. But beyond those three huge differences, hedge funds work the same way as mutual funds. We are buying into a bucket of investments that a money manager is managing, with the expectation that more of the investments will do well than those that don't, and the value of the bucket overall will increase.

Derivatives, to be blunt, are Hedge Funds on steroids. They use hedge fund money, options, foreign currency exchanges, futures, and borrowed money to make enormous bets based on a very specific set of expectations. Rarely does life happen as expected, and consequently many derivative investments fail to deliver. When we read an article about someone trying to "corner a market" they likely were using derivatives, and they are also likely going to jail.

All of these investments require an intense understanding of not only the stocks we are trading, but the market, the economics, the economies, and the assumptions it is trading in. We have to be able to predict not only what the investment is going to do, but how the market is going to react. They are generally well beyond the skill level of a normal investor, and even most financial advisors.

We have all tossed around a baseball or football in the backyard or at the beach. It is one of summer's joys. Many of us (speaking largely for the guys now – but happily for a growing number of women) have dreamed of taking a shot in the professional baseball or football leagues. We have imagined the trumpets and angelic choir in the background as we hit that walk-off grand slam or score the winning touchdown. Most of us are also smart enough to realize that performing at that level of peak physical conditioning is beyond our mere mortal abilities.

Professional athletes don't get to this level of physical fitness by engaging in a traditional strength training program or by logging a few cardio sessions a week. They push their bodies well beyond the normal physical workout to include oxygen deprivation to improve cardiovascular endurance, precision nutrition diets for muscle mass, and virtual stimulation response to improve reaction time. Under the careful and watchful eye of coaches, trainers, dieticians, nutritionists, and even medical personnel, professional athletes enhance their workouts to achieve an elite level of human performance.[2]

Unlike the exotic investments described earlier, these extreme training conditions won't just cause us to lose our investment, without proper supervision, this level of physical training can in some cases cost us our life.

Chapter 9 Easy Learning concepts:

9. *Fiscal – That which we do not fully understand can hurt us.*
9. *Physical – An exercise regimen that we do not fully understand can hurt us to the point of serious injury.*

CHAPTER 10

Other Investments: Real Estate and Annuities

No book on savings and investing would be complete without at least addressing two of the other most popular investments: **REAL ESTATE** and **ANNUITIES**. Many millennials don't want to own their own home, unlike their parents or grandparents before them. The freedom to come and go on a moment's notice has a value that they don't want to forgo. Other's struggle with owning an electronic certificate (most shares of stock are now kept digitally instead of in paper form) representing some fractional ownership percentage in a company... and see real estate as the only tangible investment worth making. Both points of view have validity.

Like with any of the investments we have already discussed, it is important to understand why we are making the investment, how it is going to make us money, and how the market works.

Buying real estate to create a passive stream of income (like a bond or CD) is not an unreasonable idea. To invest in real estate, we should make sure we factor in not only the acquisition costs, but also maintenance, marketing, taxes, and some level of breakage (un-rented space) versus what the market will bear in terms of rents.

Buying real estate to appreciate (with the goal of selling it later at a profit) is another reasonable idea, but we should be wary that real estate market cycles often take much longer than stock or bond cycles. Following the 2008 Great Recession, most real estate markets took 9 years to recover to pre-2008 levels while the stock market was back within 24 months.[1] People who had to liquidate their real estate investments following 2008 often found themselves underwater, which led to a glut of foreclosed properties pulling down the price of real estate investments that were above water. It is important to acknowledge our timelines and that we might take a loss if we are forced to sell in a down cycle.

Finally, the issues of liquidity and diversification are even more pronounced in real estate. Liquidity is how fast we can turn an investment into cash. With most stocks and bonds, we can get your money back within days, while a real estate investment may take months. How long can we wait to get our cash? And just like we wouldn't put all of our investment dollars into one stock... putting all of our investment dollars into real estate makes us susceptible to a market cycle that can seriously impact our portfolio value.

Likewise, annuities are, under the right circumstances, reasonable investments. Annuities are often sold as "Guaranteed Income For Life" and by a technical, legal definition, they are just that.

With an annuity, we give a company (generally an insurance company) our money for a period of time (the capitalization period). That annuity will grow. Here we are going to stop and take a breath, because the next concept is complicated and is critical to understanding if you ever consider purchasing an annuity. The annuity will grow – against TWO wholly separate measuring sticks.

The first measuring stick is the **ANNUITY VALUE**. This is the growth that we are provided or guaranteed in the annuity contract. For example, the contract may guarantee that if the stock market performs less than 5.0%, we are guaranteed 'at least' 5.0% growth on our Annuity Value. Other common examples are that we may get the highest growth of the market for the year, meaning that if the stock market reaches a peak of 15.0% growth during the year, and then slides back to end the year at 10.0% growth, our Annuity Value will increase by 15.0%. Both of these enticements seem attractive and are technically and legally true... However, that is ONLY if we annuitize the contract, that is, start accepting payouts from the annuity company that will last the rest of our life.

The second measuring stick is the **CASH VALUE**. This is the value if we don't want to accept payments from the annuity company, we just want to get our money back. The cash value tracks against the markets (either up or down) and may have fees and penalties baked into it.

Let's look at a simple annuity example: we invest $100,000 in an annuity with a 5.0% guarantee over the capitalization (or growth) period and a 7.0% payout. The stock market loses 10.0% during the same period of time, and the annuity has a **SURRENDER SCHEDULE** of 10%, 7%, 5%, and 3%.

Our Annuity Value will be $105,000 at the end of the first year. It is simply our $100,000 investment plus, because the stock market was less than positive 5.0%, our guaranteed 5.0% return. If we want to annuitize (start getting cash payouts that last our lifetime) the annuity company will base those payouts on the $105,000 and pay us 7.0% or $7,350 every year for the rest of our life.

Our Cash Value (if we wanted/needed to get our money back) is going to be $100,000 minus 10.0% for the stock market losses during the year, minus another 10.0% for surrendering the annuity during its first year. We will likely only get back around $81,000.

Additionally, what if we die after the first annuity payout? Yes, our annuity grew to $105,000. And yes, the company paid us 7.0% ($7,350) as they were contractually obligated to while we were alive, but what about the remaining money? Well, it can be either returned to our heirs as a death benefit or paid out to another member of our family as a continuing annuity, but ONLY if we paid extra money and bought the appropriate 'riders' (amendments to the contract). The insurance companies have a lot of smart statistician Ph.D.'s calculating down to the day when we are expected to die. They are counting on (literally betting on) us dying before we want to.

In prior chapters, we have made casual allusions to diet, rest, and stress. There is no better place than here to dive a little deeper into the relationship between physical fitness and nutrition, good sleeping patterns, and a happy mindset.

All living things (and some inanimate ones) need fuel to operate. The higher the quality of the fuel and the greater the quantity, the better the machine operates. The human body is just a machine. Excess quantities of alcohol, sugary snacks, and fatty foods will power the body with just the basics needed to sustain operation. In the case of sugar, that which isn't consumed immediately quickly turns to fat and gathers at the most inopportune locations. Fatty foods float around in our bloodstream and clog arteries.

Fad diets, promoting either eating only kale or eating only red meat, confuse the body. Unable to find balanced nutrition, the body fills in the missing nutrients from fat stores in the body, and weight loss slows. That reason alone drives the initial success that many of these diets achieve. Sadly, once the diet period is over, the body is now conditioned to believe that it may happen again, and when your food consumption returns to normal, the body will secretly squirrel away nutrients in case it needs them again.[2] And your weight and shape balloon right back up to where they began and often even bigger. Thus the term 'yo-yo dieting'.

Balanced meals of vegetables, starches, and proteins remain the best combination of fuels for our bodies. Irregular intermittent fasting does help burn off some stored nutrients, but the fasting must be done in such a way as to not scare the body into storing everything it can. There is evidence that eating heavier earlier in the day and lighter later in the day does align your fueling with exertion, preventing the storage of too many nutrients.[3]

Just as the body needs fuel, it needs rest. A healthy, regular sleep schedule built around 7 to 9 hours for adults gives the body time to repair itself from the daily exertion.[4] We have laughed at people who have told us stories about their sleep bank: deprive themselves of sleep all week long (make withdrawals from the bank) only to catch up on the weekends by sleeping the whole day (make deposits). There is no scientific evidence that suggests that this pattern does anything but leave you underpowered during the week.

In fact, lack of sleep is one of the silent but largest contributors to stress. When the body is weak from poor fuel and tired from lack of sleep, the body is much more susceptible to outside triggers. Stress and the hormone cortisol, which the body creates to soothe the frayed nerves, are known to cause nutrient storage (ie: storing fat).[5]

No health plan is complete without being aware of these three factors and following good habits. Without the fuel, energy, and right mindset, an exercise regimen will have to work harder to be effective.

Chapter 10 Easy Learning concepts:

10. *Fiscal – Real Estate and/or annuities are not unreasonable investments if used in the right way.*
10. *Physical – Ignoring nutrition, sleep, and stress levels makes our fitness success harder to achieve.*

CHAPTER 11

Beware the Get-Rich-Quick Schemes

Let's face it, hard work is, by its very definition, hard. Who among us hasn't looked for a short cut or an easier way to get our chores finished? When it comes to saving and investing (or fitness), that same desire is our enemy. Wouldn't it be great if we could double our money faster? Doubling it with taking even fewer risks would be even better. But, when tempted to cut corners or being presented with a sure-fire investment, we should ask ourselves if it really was this easy, why isn't everyone doing it?

Lots of investments argue that they will provide awesome gains in short periods of time. The Sunday paper here in Southern California is full of investment advertisements guaranteeing 8.0% plus returns with little to no risk.[1] Our guidance and best teaching for you on this is simple, yet bears repeating several times throughout this chapter: if it seems too good to be true... it probably is... and most of these investments are a bad call. Don't allow our desire to cut a corner let us fall victim to unscrupulous scam artists looking to separate us from our hard-earned money.

Some additional investments in this category may include: private placement/limited partnerships, penny stocks, life settlements, mortgage-backed trusts, timeshares, and bitcoin. We are NOT saying that every investment in the list IS a scam, just that these investments have a higher percentage of being a scam because they are largely un-/under-regulated, and un-savvy investors often lose their money because they did not fully understand the fine print of what they were investing in. When someone approaches us about an opportunity and uses any of the following words, please use caution:

- **PRIVATE PLACEMENT** – investment generally as a limited partner (limited because they want our money, but don't want to give us any say in the operations) in a smaller company. This is how many giant companies started, with a handful of faithful investors. Think about how Bill Gates moved out of his garage and built the company known today as Microsoft. Many small companies don't make it, and the chances of us getting in on the next Microsoft are remote.

- **PENNY STOCKS** – stocks trading below $1.00 in share value. Little movements in the stock price can make the stock seem like it's on its way to exploding into riches, but are often so thinly traded that we won't be able to sell our shares without depressing the price.
- **LIFE SETTLEMENTS** – let's face it, we are ALL going to die. There are legal ways to invest in a person's death and bet on when they are going to die. If we bet right, we get to collect their life insurance benefits and capture a gain versus the price we paid. If we bet wrong, then we often pay far too much for the life insurance proceeds and could capture better returns in less time in the traditional stock market.
- **MORTGAGE-BACKED TRUSTS (MBTs)** – if real estate is an investment option, then pooling our money with other like-minded people can facilitate us buying bigger or more properties as a group. Often the rub with MBTs is that we cannot sell out of them if we need/want to. They often have restrictions in the contracts that lock up our money for a period of time or limit the ways we can sell our assets (often only back to the Trust at a reduced rate).
- **TIMESHARES** – Ah... the idea of having a week at the beach in an exclusive resort

seems so enticing. We may be reading this book from the hammock or pool chair at our timeshare right now. The palm trees and heated pool call us like a siren's song. Timeshares represent, at the end of the day, the most expensive hotel room the average American will ever stay in. After our share of property taxes, maintenance fees, building assessments, and usage charges, the average timeshare runs between $275-$350 per night in annual cost.[2] That combined with the fact that we are stuck going to the same place over and over, year after year, and the costs and hassles to get out of a timeshare contract, make it less attractive.

- **BITCOIN** – What to say? Regardless of your politics, would you rather trust the federal government to manage the value of your money, or some 14-year-old computer hacker in Upper Albania? Digital money replacing paper money does seem to be the future, but at the end of the day, the organization guaranteeing the value of that digital currency needs to be someone trustworthy.

Most financial advisors don't understand the nuances of these investments either, so counting on our financial coach to guide us may be a risk in itself. Don't let Fear Of Missing Out (FOMO) drive our investment decisions. Stick with the traditional investment forms and you will be fine.

Late-night television is an awful, nay, horrible invention. We state that without hesitation or mental reservation. The products advertised at 2:00 in the morning make us wonder how, as a society, we have gotten to this point without owning every single one of the advertised gizmos and gadgets. Neither of us being psychologists, we do suppose that if you are awake at 2:00 am, it's probably because we have some gnawing concern in the back of our mind preventing us from restful sleep. And what better time to be presented with an alternative solution that can make our lives easier in just three easy payments?

In the last decade, the late-night advertisements have included products that electrocute your core muscles for a fitter, firmer stomach, weights that shake themselves (with 4 AA batteries sold separately), a stationary bicycle that will require a monthly payment equal to that of a new car, and a wearable space-aged trash bag to help us sweat out the water weight. Why, you ask, are these things even around? Well, like in investing (and in life), people are looking for a short cut to get results and these products promise more results in half the time with a quarter the effort.

If it sounds too good to be true, it probably is. There is a reason we don't find a single one of these gimmicks when we step inside a gym. It is because many trainers agree that they do not work. Outside of late-night commercial television, we will be hard-pressed to see any person serious about their fitness use these products. Not once have we met a professional personal trainer who has used these fitness gimmicks for themselves, or with one of their clients.

Advertisers specifically market these devices to the emotional vulnerability of people who are inexperienced with fitness. They are preying on our hard-earned dollars by catching us at a moment of weakness (and sleep deprivation).

Despite all these fancy so-called fitness tools and special get-fit-fast gimmicks, when it comes to long term sustainable results, there is no substitute for a quality exercise routine. We all have subconsciously shelled out hundreds of dollars buying an impulse item and/or mindless snack food. A smaller investment could be made in a professional trainer who would help us feel and look better, while possibly even helping us reduce medical costs in the future.[3]

Picking up a trash bag in a curl on garbage night or riding a $100 bike from Walmart accomplishes the same goals as the items we saw advertised, while offering the additional benefit of fresh air.

While many would have us believe that there are short cuts to wealth or health, the truth is that there is no substitution for hard work.

Chapter 11 Easy Learning concepts:

11. *Fiscal – If something is presented as such a great investment, think about why everyone else isn't doing it.*
11. *Physical – A get-fit-quick gimmick is no substitute for a quality exercise routine.*

Chapter 12

Pulling it All Together

Congratulations are in order. Together we have just completed a book on two tough topics that many people think they know, but few truly understand. You are now more knowledgeable than approximately 80% of your fellow citizens. The concepts weren't all that easy and your determination and stick-to-it-ness are to be applauded. Hopefully you have gained a certain level of respect for the many individuals who have chosen to make either finance or fitness their career.

To recap, we investigated the benefits of working with a professional, whether financial or fitness, and we developed some questions to ask ourselves when selecting the right individual to work with. Remember to not let fancy designations or swanky facilities drive your decisions, we want someone who is knowledgeable, current, and dedicated to our performance and goals.

We reviewed the three basic levels of both investing and fitness. In our investment portfolio, holding money as cash, lending it to someone, or buying something were likened to strength training, endurance, and flexibility in our exercise regimen. Hopefully, Vince's "Motion is lotion" will stick with you for quite some time.

We touched upon some higher-level concepts and legitimate alternatives to either round out our portfolio or exercise plan. Options, futures, and hedge funds can help take our portfolio to the next level, while real estate and annuities have their place in a balanced, diversified portfolio. By the same token, highly specialized training is needed to take our physical performance to the professional level and medically-based rehabilitation can reduce pain, impact of disease, and in some cases, add years and quality to our lives.

And finally, we covered some of the most common scams. Let's leave that summary with the idea that there will always be someone out there trying to separate us from our money. Don't let it be because we tried to cut a corner and allowed ourselves to be a victim. If an investment or fitness idea seems too good to be true, then it probably is.

Now it is time to pull it all together and build both an investment portfolio and exercise regimen framework that we can actually use. By reviewing the tools we've learned in the previous chapters and adhering to the following recipe, we are confident you will quickly see results:

Finance
- Start with a savings plan and build an emergency fund.
- Grow beyond saving to investing by identifying and working with a qualified financial advisor.
- Why try to pick the single winning stock or bond with our first dollar? Consider mutual funds or ETFs to spread the risk and benefit from being in many stocks or bonds at the same time. Shoot for 50.0% of the portfolio in mutual funds or ETFs.
- Add individual stocks or bonds based on your own level of aggressiveness. Whether you should be aggressive and consider adding growth stocks, or conservative and add treasury bonds to your portfolio depends on you.
- Diversify your investments so that all your eggs aren't in just one basket. Invest in companies that you know, understand, and trust, and stay informed as to how they are doing.
- Don't be afraid to sell and/or buy new investments if your life situation or goals change. Remember, it's a marathon, not a sprint.

Fitness

- The first step in a physical exercise regimen is to get up off the couch. Simple body-weight exercises, like walking around the block, loosen our joints and muscles.
- Identify and engage a certified professional trainer to avoid injury, and develop and document a plan to accomplish your goals.
- Add weights in increasing levels of difficulty to activate the muscles and stretch them beyond their comfort zone.
- Introduce complex, multi-dimensional movements to build core strength and work on balance and agility.
- Pay attention to sleep, nutrition, and stress levels, as each will increase or decrease your performance and results.
- There are no short cuts, peak performance and results come from hard work.

Hopefully, we also piqued your interest in learning more. As we promised in the foreword to this book, we covered a wide range of topics, but didn't get too deep. Truthfully, there are many books dedicated to each of the concepts we covered all the way up to the most scholarly of tomes. If you found a topic that interests you, we hope you will continue your learning and asking questions.

The Boldface Summary

Chapter	Fiscal Fitness Rules	Physical Fitness Rules
1. IT'S ALL REALLY EASY	If we want to save money, then we MUST spend less than we make.	If we want to lose weight, then we MUST burn more calories than we consume.
2. THE BENEFITS OF WORKING WITH A PROFESSIONAL	The 3 D's and a professional advisor can help us reach our investing goals.	The 3 D's and a professional trainer can help us achieve our health goals.
3. PICKING THE RIGHT PROFESSIONAL	Seek an Advisor that shares your philosophy and is willing to work with you as a fiduciary, regardless of fancy-sounding designations.	Find a Certified Personal Trainer who has expertise with your specific needs and is compatible with your personality.
4. START EARLY: PAY IT NOW OR PAY IT LATER	The Rule of 72 helps us find the time and rate we need to double our money.	3,500 calories are equal to one pound of fat. We need to 'cut' or 'burn' those calories to lose weight.
5. GETTING STARTED	There are only 3 things we can do with our money to make it grow: hold as cash, lend, or buy.	There are really only 3 types of activities that we can do to improve our health: strength, endurance, and flexibility.

6. BEGINNER LEVEL: CASH	Cash is King, but no more than 6 to 9 months in an emergency fund.	Establish a daily routine that focuses on form and technique.
7. INTERMEDIATE LEVEL: LENDING AND BONDS	We can lend our money in a contract called a Bond.	Progressively incorporating more complex exercises raises the return on our physical investment.
8. ADVANCED LEVEL: MUTUAL FUNDS, ETFs, AND INDIVIDUAL STOCKS	Buying a stock is a complicated decision not to be contemplated simply because a buddy recommended it, but mutual funds and ETFs can help spread the risk of picking losers.	We need to increase dynamic demands on our muscles to continue seeing results.
9. EXPERT LEVEL: OPTIONS, FUTURES, AND HEDGE FUNDS	That which we do not fully understand can hurt us.	An exercise regimen that we do not fully understand can hurt us to the point of serious injury.
10. OTHER INVESTMENTS: REAL ESTATE AND ANNUITIES	Real Estate and/or annuities are not unreasonable investments if used in the right way.	Ignoring nutrition, sleep, and stress levels makes our fitness success harder to achieve.
11. BEWARE THE GET-RICH-QUICK SCHEMES	If something is presented as such a great investment, think about why everyone else isn't doing it.	A get-fit-quick gimmick is no substitute for a quality exercise routine.

Citations

Chapter 1
1. Savings Rate Data: Statista.com // Inflation Rate Data: Bureau of Labor Statistics, Consumer Price Index data (1960-2019) as published at usinflationcalculator.com
2. "What Percentage of Americans Owns Stock?", Lydia Saad, Gallup News, Sept 13, 2019
3. Home Ownership Data: US Census Bureau data as presented by fred.StLouisFed.org
4. "70% of American Investors Wished They Had Handled Their Money Differently in 2019", Anna Hecht, CNBC, Dec 28, 2019
5. Mercer's 2019/2020 US Compensation Planning Survey
6. NHANES Obesity data: published by the Center for Disease Control at cdc.gov/nchs/data/hestat/obesity

Chapter 2

1. Calculation performed on $6,000 annual contribution during periods 1 through 10, versus through periods 11 through 44 at 7.0% average interest rate
2. "2 Forms of Exercise Are the Best Way to Stave Off The Effects of Aging...", Erin Brodwin, Business Insider, Sep 8, 2018
3. Report On Injury Origination, www.FitnessPerscriptions.com
4. "The Pros and Cons of Hiring a Financial Advisor", Abby Hayes, US News and World Report, Jul 20, 2016

Chapter 3

1. www.HolidayInn.com
2. "Prelicensing Program Requirements", www.Insurance.ca.gov
3. www.CFP.net
4. "Insight: When Precedent Doesn't Really Stand...", Rubin, Giffin, and Fox, Bloomberg Law, Dec 12, 2018
5. "Top 5 Best Personal Trainer Certification Programs...", www.BecomingATrainer.com

Chapter 4

1. "Einstein and Compound Interest", www.Snopes.com
2. "Did Einstein Invent the Rule of 72?", www.ColorAccounting.com, Jun 28, 2017

Citations

3. Average Salary Data: Bureau of Labor Statistics
4. "New IRS Distributional Data on The Federal Income Tax", Erica York, www.TaxFoundation.org, Oct 17, 2019
5. Average State Income Tax Rates range from 0.0% in Texas and Nevada up to 13.0% in California. Some states have flat taxes, while others use a progressive tax and still others hide their taxing through sales, local and property tax plans. We use 2.0% for ease of calculation.
6. "How Frugal Are You? Compare Your Monthly Expenses to The Average", Amy Fontinelle, reprinted in The Motley Fool, Jan 21, 2020
7. Annual Costs of Pet Ownership data from ASPCA, David Weliver, www.MoneyUnder30.com, Apr 27, 2020
8. Inflation Rate Data: Bureau of Labor Statistics, Consumer Price Index data (1960-2019) as published at usinflationcalculator.com
9. Dow Jones Average since 2000 data: www.YahooFinance.com
10. S&P500 Average since 2000 data: www.YahooFinance.com
11. 2015-2020 Dietary Guidelines Table A2-1, www.USDA.gov
12. "6 Charts That Show How Much More Americans Eat...", Skye Gould, Business Insider, May 10, 2017

Chapter 5
1. "Study: Checking Fees Average Almost $1,000...", www.NerdWallet.com
2. The Mamba Mentality: How I Play, Kobe Bryant, Farrar, Straus, and Giroux, Oct 2018

Chapter 6
1. "Understanding Deposit Insurance", www.FDIC.gov

Chapter 7
1. "Explainer: How Does Negative Interest Rate Policy Work?", Reuters, Sep 13, 2019
2. 10 Year Treasury Rate – 54 Year Historical Chart, www.MacroTrends.com
3. "Municipal Bonds and Historical Calendar Year Returns, Thomas Kenny, www.TheBalance.com, Oct 29, 2019
4. Moody's Seasoned Baa Corporate Bond Yield, fred.StLouisFed.org
5. "One Country, Nine Defaults: Argentina is Caught in a Vicious Cycle", Bartenstein, Maki and Gertz, Bloomberg News, May 24, 2020

Chapter 8
1. "World's Oldest Stock Certificate Found", Xinhua News, Sep 10, 2010

2. How Many Shares Does a Company Have? Everything You Need To Know, www.UpCounsel.com
3. "Many Investors Don't Know the Difference Between Mutual Funds and ETFs...", Sarah O'Brien, CNBC, Oct 5, 2018
4. Morning Star Style Boxes
5. "The Real Reason Value Has Been Lagging Growth", Julie Segal, www.InstitutionalInvestor.com, Oct 24, 2019
6. Ibid.
7. VIX Average since 2000 data: www.YahooFinance.com
8. PE Ratio By Sector (US), www.Stern.NYU.edu, as of January 2020

Chapter 9

1. "Power Line: The Real Reason Crude Oil Went Negative...", Benji Jones, Business Insider, Apr 24, 2020
2. "The Truth About Hypoxic Training and Oxygen Reducing Masks", Anthony Roberts, www.BreakingMuscle.com

Chapter 10

1. S&P/Case Shiller US National Home Price Index vs ^DJIA
2. "Why Diets Don't Actually Work...", Roberto Ferdman, Washington Post, May 2015

3. Ibid.
4. "Sleep Needs", www.WebMD.com
5. "What is Cortisol", www.Hormone.org

Chapter 11
1. LA Times – Business Section, May 31, 2020
2. "The True Cost of Owning a Timeshare", www.TimeshareExitTeam.com
3. "Exercising Can Help You Keep Medical Costs Down", American Heart Association, Journal of the American Heart Association, Sept 7, 2016

About the Authors

Mr. Fellows grew up wanting to be an X-wing fighter pilot ever since he saw Star Wars in 1977. Unable to find a reasonable career path to such a position, he satisfied himself with a 22-year career in corporate finance, rising to the level of CFO before retiring in 2011. He holds a Master's of Business Administration and is currently mid-way through his Juris Doctorate. Bored in retirement, he picked up a private pilot's license, a boat, a motorcycle, became a volunteer fireman, and ran Ironman's 1/2Kona Triathlon to while away the time. Mr. Fellows finally opened his own firm to work with the greatly underserved investor who was too small to garner the attention of Wall Street professionals, and too large to benefit from the local cookie-cutter wirehouses. Today, Fellows Wealth Management is a family office in Irvine, California.

Mr. Levigne always dreamed of being a rock-star. Unfortunately, serious underestimating the amount of skill required to play the "air guitar" and general tone-deafness assured that his debut concert would also be his farewell performance. He then went on to combine his passions as an educator with a love of physical fitness. After his Master's degree, Mr. Levigne taught elementary and high school physical education and coached a number of football teams in Michigan. Tired of the cold winters, he relocated to Southern California where he holds medical and orthopedic training certificates, continues to teach and mentor at-risk high school youth, and serves as CEO of FitScripts, a company designed specifically to help those with medical conditions integrate a work out regimen applicable to their ailments.

Mr. Levigne also rehabilitated Mr. Fellows' knee after a freak golfing accident and most days they can be found together in the gym at 06:00 am.